BLOOD AT THE BORDER

The Murder of Amber Hagerman

Linda Davidson

For Amber— whose light still cuts through every darkness, whose name still saves the lost. And for every parent who has ever waited by the window, listening for a sound that never came— this is for you.

For every child who should have been safe, and for every stranger who refused to look away.

CONTENTS

AUTHOR'S NOTE

This book was written with deep respect for the Hagerman family, the investigators who carried this case through the decades, and every community that has stood guard over its children since.

The facts in this narrative are drawn from official reports, public records, law enforcement accounts, and media archives. Dialogue and scenes are reconstructed through verified testimony and contemporary interviews. Some conversations and descriptions have been dramatized for clarity and readability, but the truth — the brutal, unrelenting truth — remains unchanged.

At its heart, *Blood at the Border* is not only the story of a crime.

It is the story of what the world became because of it.

INTRODUCTION

—The Day the World
Stopped Listening

January 13, 1996. Arlington, Texas.

A quiet Saturday afternoon. Two children ride their bikes through a forgotten parking lot behind an old Winn-Dixie grocery store.

Eight seconds later, one of them is gone.

The abduction and murder of **nine-year-old Amber Hagerman** shocked the nation not simply because of its cruelty, but because of its clarity. The crime happened in broad daylight. There was a witness. A vehicle description. A neighborhood full of people. And still, the man who took her disappeared — as if the world blinked at the wrong moment.

That failure — the silence between the scream and the search — exposed something terrifying: in 1996, America had no rapid way to warn its citizens that a child had been taken.

Out of that silence, a revolution began.

This is the story of how a single crime ignited one of the most life-saving systems in modern history. It is also the story of the girl behind it — *the real Amber*, whose smile lit up her family's world, whose bicycle was found abandoned, and whose name now travels across continents every time a child is in danger.

It is a story of loss, of fury, of innovation born from grief.

But above all, it is a story about how even in death, a child's light refused to go out.

PROLOGUE: THE EMPTY BIKE

The afternoon light was soft that day—golden, lazy, the kind that falls gently across cracked sidewalks and old fences in a neighborhood that doesn't expect to make headlines. It was Saturday, January 13, 1996, in Arlington, Texas. The temperature hovered around sixty degrees, a brief winter reprieve that coaxed children outdoors. There was no hint in the air that this quiet stretch of East Abram Street would soon become a name seared into the national conscience.

Amber Hagerman, nine years old, pedaled her pink bicycle alongside her younger brother Ricky. They were close—inseparable, really—the kind of siblings who bickered one minute and shared cookies the next. Their grandmother's house sat just blocks away from a small, unused grocery store parking lot where local kids sometimes rode up and down the loading ramp. Amber's laughter carried across the street as her tires hummed over the pavement, her black hair flying behind her in a loose ponytail. She had no way of knowing she was crossing an invisible line—one between safety and something unspeakable.

Her brother stopped first. "Grandma said not to go too far," he reminded her. Amber waved him off, teasing, "Just a minute!" She turned her bike, looping one more time around the ramp. It was the last trace of freedom she would ever know.

A man across the street, 78-year-old Jim Kevil, was standing in his yard just a few dozen yards away. He would later tell police what he saw: a dark pickup truck, possibly black or blue, pulling suddenly into the lot. A man jumped out, broad-shouldered, maybe in his twenties or thirties. The struggle was brief, frantic— a flash of movement, a cry that didn't last long enough. Then the truck was gone, tires squealing as it turned sharply and vanished down the street.

Kevil ran inside, shouting for his wife to call 911. Within minutes, Arlington police were on their way, and within an hour, the lot swarmed with officers, neighbors, and frantic relatives. But Amber's bicycle—the small pink one with white handles and scuffed paint—remained propped on its side, one wheel still slowly spinning in the winter air.

The news spread through the neighborhood like fire through dry grass. Amber's mother, Donna, arrived within minutes, disbelief overtaking panic. She'd left her children in the care of her mother just hours earlier, trusting that the day would be as ordinary as any other. When she saw the empty lot cordoned off by yellow tape and her daughter's bike abandoned on the pavement, her knees buckled. That image—so ordinary, yet so final—became a living nightmare no mother could ever wake from.

By sundown, local news stations had broken the story. "Nine-year-old Amber Hagerman abducted in broad daylight," the headlines read. Volunteers gathered at a nearby church, forming search parties with flashlights and maps. Parents hugged their children tighter that night. Strangers stood outside their homes staring into the dark, as if watching might somehow bring her back.

The FBI was called in within hours, the speed of their involvement a measure of the horror. Agents canvassed the neighborhood, taking statements, building timelines. The abduction had lasted no more than eight seconds, but those eight seconds shattered a community's sense of safety.

The following days blurred into each other—searches, press conferences, leads that evaporated. Helicopters thumped overhead. Canine units combed fields and drainage ditches. Hundreds of volunteers trudged through brush and trash-strewn lots. Each day that passed made hope feel thinner, stretched to the breaking point.

On the fourth day, hope broke completely.

A man walking his dog along a nearby creek spotted something that didn't belong—a shape tangled in reeds. Police arrived within minutes, and soon the area filled with flashing lights and murmured orders. What they found confirmed every parent's worst fear. Amber Hagerman's body lay in shallow water, discarded less than five miles from where she had been taken. The cause of death was later ruled as her throat being cut.

Even the seasoned investigators fell silent.

The media storm that followed was unlike anything Arlington had seen. Reporters swarmed the scene, cameras rolling as officers worked, though few words could capture the brutality of what had been done. The story made national news within a day. Talk shows debated safety, neighborhood watch programs, and what kind of monster could do such a thing.

But beneath the noise and outrage was a quieter current—grief, raw and personal. Donna Hagerman sat for interviews not to feed the cameras, but because she wanted people to remember her daughter's face. "She was just a little girl," she told one reporter, her voice breaking. "She didn't do anything wrong. She was just riding her bike."

Amber became a symbol overnight, though no mother ever asks for her child to be turned into a symbol. Her picture —a bright-eyed fourth grader with a missing front tooth— appeared everywhere. Flyers covered telephone poles, grocery store windows, school bulletin boards. And as days turned into weeks and then months, the case went cold. No one was arrested.

The man in the dark pickup vanished as completely as if the earth had swallowed him.

Still, the image of that empty bike lingered—a small, wordless reminder of the moment innocence was snatched from a street in Texas.

Yet, from that loss came something the world would not forget.

In the wake of Amber's murder, local radio and police began talking about how quickly information could have been spread if there had been a way to alert the public immediately. A Dallas-Fort Worth broadcaster suggested creating a rapid child-abduction alert system. It was called, fittingly, the **AMBER Alert**—America's Missing: Broadcast Emergency Response. The name was chosen to honor the little girl whose life had been stolen in broad daylight, just a few blocks from home.

No one knew then how far that idea would reach. No one knew it would one day stretch beyond Texas, beyond borders, across the world. That from a single tragedy, thousands of children would be found, rescued, returned. But that is the paradox of Amber Hagerman's story: her death birthed a system that has saved countless others.

Today, nearly three decades later, the lot where Amber was taken still exists, though it's overgrown and mostly forgotten by passing drivers. To most, it's just another patch of cracked concrete. But for those who remember, it's sacred ground—a reminder of how swiftly evil can move, and how stubbornly love fights back.

Some who lived nearby still remember that Saturday afternoon. They recall the sound of sirens, the confusion, the way time seemed to stop. For Amber's family, the years have not dulled the pain. Her case remains open, a haunting question without an answer: **Who killed Amber Hagerman?**

Every so often, new leads surface—DNA advances, re-examined evidence, whispers that the past might finally speak. But until that day comes, Amber's legacy lives on in every emergency alert that flashes across a phone, every broadcast interrupting music or news to announce that another child is missing.

Each time, the words appear: *An AMBER Alert has been issued.*

Each time, the world stops—just for a moment—to look, to listen, to help.

And somewhere, in the quiet, a pink bicycle stands still, its wheel turning slowly in the wind, waiting for the day justice finally catches up.

CHAPTER 1 AMBER — A PORTRAIT IN MOTION

Before Amber Hagerman became a name spoken in sorrow, she was just a little girl who loved to ride fast.

Her world was small, ordinary, and filled with all the things that make up a child's universe: the thrill of a bike with streamers on the handlebars, the comfort of her mother's voice, the adventure of a Saturday with no homework and no limits. The Hagermans lived in Arlington, Texas—a working-class suburb wedged between Dallas and Fort Worth—where backyards smelled of cut grass, chain-link fences separated neighbors, and the air in summer hummed with the sound of cicadas.

To the people who knew her best, Amber was a blur of energy. She was nine years old, with shoulder-length dark hair, bright brown eyes, and a smile that seemed to stretch faster than her words. "She never walked anywhere," her mother, Donna, once said. "She always ran." There was something about her—an insistence on motion, on life, as if she already knew that time was too short to waste standing still.

Amber lived with her mother Donna and her five-year-old brother Ricky in a modest duplex on Highland Drive. Donna was a single mother, working long hours at a local grocery store, holding everything together with the fierce determination that mothers often discover only when they have no other choice. The family didn't have much, but they had each other, and that was enough. When Donna worked late, her parents—Amber's grandparents, Jimmy and Glenda Whitson—watched the kids. Their house became a second home, full of warmth and discipline, of sweet tea and rules that came from love.

Amber adored her grandmother, who kept the family close and the kitchen full. On weekends, she'd help bake cookies, sneaking chocolate chips when she thought no one was looking. "She was such a helper," Glenda recalled later. "She loved to feel useful, grown-up." Amber wasn't just helpful—she was protective. If her brother fell off his bike, she'd be the first to run over, brush him off, and make sure he was okay before scolding him for being careless. "She acted like a little mother," her grandmother said.

She dreamed big, even from her small corner of Texas. One week she wanted to be a teacher, the next a country singer, and sometimes a veterinarian. Her room was a collage of dolls, crayon drawings, and taped-up posters from children's magazines. She kept her bike close, too—the same pink one she'd been riding the day she disappeared. It was her ticket to freedom, her way to explore beyond the fences and sidewalks that defined her world.

At school, she was the kind of student teachers remembered—not because she was perfect, but because she was alive in the classroom. Curious, outspoken, sometimes stubborn. She raised her hand often, not always with the right answer, but always with confidence. Her third-grade teacher once told Donna, "Amber's got a spark. She's going to make something of herself." Donna smiled at that, storing the compliment away like a small piece of hope.

Friends described her as daring. She'd jump from swings, climb trees higher than the boys, and challenge neighborhood kids to races she often won. She was fearless, even when she probably shouldn't have been. "She liked to push limits," Ricky would later say. "But she always came home when Mom said to."

Family was the axis of Amber's world. Donna was the center of it, the mother who worked late nights but always found time to tuck her kids in and tell them she loved them. Times were tough, but Donna's love was constant—steady as heartbeat. She had separated from Amber's father, Richard Hagerman, but he remained in their lives, visiting when he could. Despite the divorce, both parents adored their children deeply. Amber's world might have been modest, but it was filled with love.

They had rituals—Saturday cartoons, bike rides, visits to Grandma's house, walks to the park. Amber loved pancakes with strawberries, bubblegum ice cream, and the occasional trip to the nearby Walmart where she'd beg for sparkly hair clips or stickers. Her innocence was complete, untouched by the idea that the world could hold real monsters.

Sometimes, she'd watch the news with her grandmother, restless during the serious parts, asking questions that showed her age and innocence. "Why would someone hurt a kid?" she once asked when a story about a missing child aired. Her grandmother, caught off guard, told her not to worry—"That kind of thing doesn't happen here."

No one knew that, weeks later, it would.

The Hagermans' neighborhood was ordinary by every measure— neither dangerous nor wealthy, a place where neighbors nodded in passing but didn't lock their doors until late. Kids roamed in packs, playing tag and hide-and-seek until the porch lights flickered on. It was 1996, just before the world changed—the last breath of an era when children rode bikes without cell phones and when the biggest worry was a scraped knee, not a missing child alert flashing across a television screen.

Amber loved that freedom. It was the kind of freedom that makes childhood feel infinite. She'd ride down Highland Drive, hair whipping in the wind, laughing, calling to her brother to keep up. That bike wasn't just transportation—it was her declaration of independence.

Donna worried sometimes, but she tried to let her daughter explore. "You can't keep her locked up," she'd tell herself. "She's growing." Still, she always had one rule: *Stay close to Grandma's house.* Amber usually obeyed. Usually.

That January afternoon, Donna dropped the kids off at her mother's house before heading out for errands. It was supposed to be an easy day—routine, forgettable. The kind of day no one remembers unless it's the last one they'd ever get to live the way they used to.

In the days after Amber vanished, people searched for who she was as much as what had happened. The headlines called her "a bright, outgoing girl." The news anchors used words like "sweet," "innocent," "beloved." But the real Amber was more complex than that—she was brave, fiery, funny. She could make a room light up, but she could also dig in her heels when she didn't get her way. She was, above all, a child full of possibility, standing at the edge of everything she could one day become.

That is why her story mattered so much. Because when a child like Amber is taken, it isn't just one life stolen—it's the ripples that follow. It's the birthdays that never happen, the graduations that never come, the woman she could have grown into. It's the laughter that once echoed down the block and now lives only in memory.

To tell Amber's story is to honor all of that—the motion, the dreams, the love that filled her short life. Before she became a headline, before her name turned into an alert system, she was a girl who loved pancakes, pink bikes, and the feeling of the wind on her face.

And that is how we must remember her—not as the victim of a crime, but as the child who once lived fully, freely, and without fear.

CHAPTER 2 SATURDAY, JANUARY 13

Morning came slow that day, gentle and ordinary. The kind of Texas morning that slips through the curtains like honey—warm, bright, and deceptively peaceful. For the Hagerman family, it began as any Saturday would. No school, no rush, just the small comforts of routine. Amber woke first, padding barefoot into the kitchen where her grandmother Glenda was already fixing breakfast. The smell of bacon and biscuits filled the air.

"Morning, sunshine," Glenda said, smiling as Amber climbed onto a chair. "Hungry?"

Amber grinned, nodding. "Always."

Her younger brother Ricky soon joined them, rubbing his eyes. The two children bickered lightly over who got the bigger biscuit before dissolving into laughter. Their grandmother's house had always been a refuge—a small brick home tucked on East Abram Street, with lace curtains and the faint scent of coffee and furniture polish. It was a house built on love and predictability.

After breakfast, the kids settled into their favorite cartoons. Glenda folded laundry, humming softly to herself. Donna, their mother, called from home to check in before heading out for errands. She trusted that her children were safe here. She had no reason not to.

By midmorning, the weather turned unseasonably warm. Sixty degrees in January was a gift, and the sunlight begged to be used. Amber grew restless. "Can we ride our bikes, Grandma?" she asked, eyes bright. Glenda hesitated—she was protective, always had been—but eventually nodded. "Stay close. Don't go past the corner, you hear?"

Amber nodded eagerly, already racing to fetch her bike. Ricky followed, pulling on his sneakers. The two of them wheeled their bikes down the narrow street, the air filled with the metallic click of chains and the squeak of rubber tires.

The neighborhood was quiet that afternoon, peaceful in a way that would haunt it later. A few cars rolled by; someone was mowing their lawn down the block. The sound of children laughing drifted faintly from a nearby yard.

The siblings pedaled toward the abandoned Winn-Dixie grocery store just a few blocks away. It had been closed for years, its faded sign still clinging to the building like an echo from another time. Behind the store was a loading ramp—a makeshift playground for local kids. It was a small thrill: racing up the incline, coasting down, feeling the wind whip through your hair.

For a while, it was pure joy. Amber's laughter echoed off the empty walls, mingling with the rhythm of Ricky's pedals. She rode circles around him, calling, "Bet you can't catch me!"

"I'm telling Grandma if you go too far!" he shouted back, half-laughing, half-serious.

Amber was always braver, always the explorer. When Ricky finally turned back toward their grandmother's house, she waved him off. "One more time!" she said. Just one more.

Those were the last words her brother would ever hear her say.

Across the street, 78-year-old Jim Kevil was in his yard, tinkering with a small radio. He had lived there for decades, seen kids come and go from that parking lot for years. It was harmless—just children playing. But what he saw next would stay with him forever.

"I saw a man jump out of his truck," he would later tell police. "He ran toward her, grabbed her off the bike, and threw her into the cab. Then he drove off."

The whole thing lasted less than ten seconds.

Kevil shouted for help but was too far away. The truck—a black or dark blue pickup with a short bed—peeled out, tires screeching. He tried to chase it in his car but lost it at the next intersection. His heart pounded as he ran inside to call 911.

It was 3:18 p.m. when the first emergency call came in.

When Glenda answered the door a few minutes later, Ricky was out of breath, panic written all over his face. "They took her! A man took Amber!" he cried.

At first, the words didn't make sense. Glenda grabbed her keys and raced toward the parking lot. What she found made her knees buckle—the pink bike lying on its side near the ramp, one wheel still spinning. There was no sign of Amber.

Within minutes, Arlington police arrived. They questioned Kevil, sealed off the lot, and began the search. Officers combed nearby streets, checked ditches and driveways. Helicopters took to the air, scanning fields and alleys. Neighborhood residents spilled out of their houses, forming impromptu search parties.

Amber's mother, Donna, rushed to the scene, breathless and disoriented. "Where is she?" she demanded, but no one had an answer. A detective gently took her aside. "We're doing everything we can," he said, though his eyes betrayed the urgency in his voice.

The witnesses described the truck, the driver, the direction it went. But details were fuzzy; shock blurred everything. Some said it had a white mark on the side, others said it didn't. Some thought the driver was in his twenties, others in his forties. Every minute that passed widened the distance between what they saw and what could be proved.

By dusk, the story had already made local news. Reporters stood behind police tape as officers searched the creek bed and nearby alleys. The sun dipped low, turning the sky a deep orange that looked almost cruel against the chaos unfolding below.

Donna refused to leave. She clung to a hope only mothers can understand—that any minute, her daughter would appear, walking toward her, crying, frightened, but alive.

But night fell, and the lot grew dark.

That night, search teams fanned out across the area with flashlights, their beams cutting through fields and culverts. Volunteers brought food, maps, and flyers. Radio stations broadcast Amber's description: **"Nine years old, four feet six inches tall, dark hair, brown eyes, wearing a pink jacket and jeans."**

Tips flooded in, but most led nowhere. Someone thought they saw the truck near a highway; another said they recognized the driver's face. Police chased every lead. None panned out.

Inside the Hagerman home, the phone rang endlessly. Friends, relatives, reporters—it was a blur. Donna sat at the kitchen table, clutching a stuffed bear that had been Amber's favorite. The silence between calls was the hardest part.

"She's strong," Donna whispered to her mother. "She's my baby. She's going to come home."

Outside, the streets were lined with volunteers and police cars, the air thick with sirens and searchlight glare. But somewhere beyond that circle of light, Amber was gone.

That evening, as detectives reviewed the timeline, one fact chilled them: the entire abduction had unfolded in less than eight seconds. Eight seconds between laughter and horror. Eight seconds that no one could take back.

It was too fast to predict, too cruel to prevent. And it happened in daylight, in a residential neighborhood, under the watch of witnesses.

If a child could vanish like that here, it could happen anywhere.

By midnight, the search radius had expanded miles beyond Arlington. Patrol cars moved in convoy, scanning highways and backroads. The FBI was called in before dawn. The case had already crossed from local tragedy to national urgency.

Amber's name filled the airwaves, her photo on every news broadcast in North Texas.

But by sunrise, the pink bicycle still lay where it had fallen. Its wheel, long stopped, pointed toward the empty sky.

The silence that followed was heavy—an entire community holding its breath, waiting for the next phone call, the next lead, the next sign of hope.

No one could yet imagine how those eight seconds would echo for decades, reshaping how the world searched for its missing children.

CHAPTER 3 I SAW HIM TAKE HER

The witness who saw it happen would remember the sound first—the sudden squeal of tires, sharp and wrong against the calm of a Saturday afternoon.

Jim Kevil had lived in his home on East Abram Street for nearly thirty years. Retired, soft-spoken, the kind of neighbor who knew everyone by name, he was standing in his front yard that day, radio on low, pruning a rosebush. The Hagerman children had been riding up and down the old Winn-Dixie ramp for nearly an hour, their laughter blending with the faint hum of passing traffic.

Then, the sound changed.

Kevil looked up just as a dark truck swung into the lot, gravel spitting under its tires. The driver's door flew open. A man jumped out—white, medium build, maybe in his twenties or thirties, clean-shaven, wearing a black jacket and jeans. His movements were abrupt, practiced almost. In one motion, he grabbed Amber off her bike, lifted her, and shoved her into the cab.

"She screamed once," Kevil would later tell police. "A quick scream. Then it stopped."

He froze for half a second, his brain trying to catch up to what his eyes had just seen. Then instinct kicked in. He dropped his pruning shears and shouted for his wife to call 911. The truck peeled out, turning west down Abram before he could reach his car. He tried anyway, jumping behind the wheel and following the sound of fading tires—but by the next intersection, the truck was gone.

The entire abduction lasted **eight seconds**.

When police arrived, Kevil's front yard had already become a scene of chaos. Neighbors emerged from their houses, drawn by sirens and shouting. Glenda Whitson stood trembling beside the ramp, staring at her granddaughter's bicycle as if sheer will could make Amber appear beside it again.

An officer gently guided her back toward the sidewalk, promising they'd find her. She barely heard him. "She was just right here," she kept repeating. "She was right here."

The first officers on scene took down Kevil's statement, sketching out a crude diagram on a notepad: truck, ramp, direction of travel. They broadcast the initial description over police radio. Within minutes, patrol cars spread out like spokes from the center of a wheel—every major street, alley, and highway exit in Arlington filled with flashing blue lights.

But the suspect was already gone.

Detectives from the Arlington Police Department arrived within an hour, led by Sgt. Mike Simonds, a veteran investigator with years on the force. The first priority was containment: interview witnesses, preserve the scene, find physical evidence. But the parking lot offered little.

They marked tire impressions with chalk, photographed the bicycle, collected fibers and footprints. The truck had left a partial tire tread, but nothing distinct enough to trace. There were no cameras—this was 1996, before security systems were common. What they had were the witness's words, a few scuffs in the dirt, and an empty space where a child should have been.

Inside a makeshift command post set up at a nearby church, detectives drew up timelines. They interviewed Kevil again and again, comparing his statements with anything neighbors might have seen. Some claimed to have noticed a truck earlier that week, circling slowly, engine idling. Others weren't sure. Memory, they knew, was unreliable—especially under shock.

Kevil was certain about one thing. "She didn't get in willingly," he said. "He grabbed her."

By early evening, the FBI had been notified. Child abduction cases triggered automatic coordination between local and federal agencies. Special agents from the Dallas field office arrived within hours, bringing expertise in child abduction response.

The command center hummed with activity—maps spread across tables, phone lines blinking, coffee cooling untouched. Every tip that came in was logged, categorized, and dispatched to field teams. Leads poured in: sightings of similar trucks, strangers seen near playgrounds, even rumors from neighboring cities. Most evaporated under scrutiny.

The pressure was immense. In child abduction cases, every minute mattered. Research showed that the first three hours were the most critical; beyond that, the odds of recovery dropped sharply.

By nightfall, detectives had followed dozens of leads. None had found Amber.

Back at the Whitson home, the mood was unbearable. Reporters had gathered outside, cameras flashing each time the door opened. Donna Hagerman stood in the living room surrounded by relatives, her face pale, eyes rimmed red. She held Ricky close, his small body trembling in her arms.

He kept saying the same thing: "She said she'd be right back."

Donna stroked his hair, trying to steady her voice. "It's okay, baby. We're going to find her."

But when the police returned that evening to brief the family, their words were careful, measured. There were no breakthroughs. No suspect in custody. Only a vehicle description —a dark pickup with a short bed—and a rough sketch based on Kevil's account.

It wasn't much, but it was something.

The sketch artist worked late into the night at the station, translating fragments of memory into a face. Kevil closed his eyes, trying to recall every detail—the curve of the man's jaw, the cut of his hair, the way he moved. "It happened so fast," he said again and again. "I can't be sure."

The finished sketch was released the next morning: a composite of a young white male, medium build, short dark hair. The image hit local news by noon, and soon, it was everywhere.

Tips began flooding in—hundreds by the end of the weekend. People thought they recognized the man from the sketch, or they'd seen a similar truck parked behind a gas station, or near the interstate, or by a park. Police chased every lead, their hope rising and falling with each call.

In the command center, maps of Arlington were now covered in colored pins—each one a tip, a direction, a possibility. Detectives were running on adrenaline and bad coffee. They knew they were in a race not just against time, but against fear itself.

Still, even as the trail cooled, Kevil's words haunted them.

"I saw him take her."

There was no doubt in his mind about what he'd seen. But there was also no trace—no fingerprints, no witnesses beyond him, no one who could confirm the truck's direction after it left Abram Street. It was as if the man and the child had vanished into the air.

That night, Donna couldn't sleep. She sat by the window, watching the flashing lights outside fade as patrol cars rotated shifts. She replayed every moment of that day—the breakfast, the laughter, the goodbyes. If she had come five minutes earlier, if she had said "no bikes today," if she had just held them home a little longer.

Guilt is cruel that way. It always rewrites time.

In the quiet, she whispered a prayer she'd whisper many times again over the years:

"Please, God. Just bring her home."

Outside, the wind stirred the trees. The pink bicycle had been taken into evidence, but in Donna's mind, she could still see it —lying there in the parking lot, the wheel spinning, waiting for someone who would never return.

Eight seconds.

One witness.

One truck.

And a family that would never be the same.

CHAPTER 4 THE FIRST 24 HOURS

The night after Amber Hagerman was taken, Arlington, Texas, was not the same town it had been that morning.

The air itself felt different—thicker, charged with fear and urgency. In the dark, flashlights cut across vacant lots and backyards. Search dogs barked into the wind, their handlers straining to hear something—anything—beyond the buzz of radios and the low hum of engines.

Somewhere out there was a nine-year-old girl, missing for less than twelve hours, and everyone knew that the first day might decide everything.

The command post at a nearby Baptist church buzzed like a war room. Phones rang non-stop. Volunteers crowded in, signing their names on yellow legal pads. The smell of coffee and damp paper filled the air. Detectives mapped out grids on chalkboards, assigning search teams by block and direction.

Sgt. Mike Simonds coordinated the efforts with precision born from experience. He knew that statistically, if a child wasn't found within the first twenty-four hours, the chances of recovery dropped sharply. He didn't say it out loud, but everyone in that room felt it.

By midnight, over one hundred volunteers were searching. They combed through empty lots, drainage ditches, creeks, and wooded patches. Police cruisers crawled down alleys, their spotlights scanning fences and abandoned sheds. Helicopters circled overhead, their beams sweeping across the sleeping city.

From above, Arlington looked like a patchwork of light and shadow—each beam of a flashlight representing hope refusing to die.

At the Whitson home, the Hagerman family waited. The front door was never fully closed—neighbors and friends came and went, bringing casseroles, flashlights, hugs that couldn't help. The living room was quiet except for the murmur of the TV, tuned to the latest news update.

Donna sat near the window, her eyes fixed on the dark street beyond. She hadn't slept, hadn't eaten. Her hands trembled as she clutched Amber's favorite stuffed bear—a white rabbit with worn ears. "She's going to walk through that door," she kept saying softly, more to herself than anyone else.

Her mother, Glenda, tried to stay strong, but tears kept slipping down her cheeks. "We'll find her, honey," she whispered. "We'll find her."

Every knock on the door jolted them upright. Each phone call carried the weight of life or death.

By dawn, reporters were already outside. News vans lined the street, their satellite dishes pointed skyward. Cameras filmed volunteers leaving for another round of searches. Amber's photo —her school portrait, smiling in a white shirt and denim vest— was now everywhere. It was printed on hundreds of flyers, each one bearing the same desperate plea:

MISSING: AMBER RENÉ HAGERMAN, AGE 9

Last seen: 3:18 p.m., January 13, Arlington, TX.

If you have any information, call the Arlington Police Department.

Volunteers handed them out at gas stations, grocery stores, laundromats. Cashiers taped them to registers. Strangers took stacks to post around their neighborhoods.

For once, no one was a stranger.

At police headquarters, the investigation was already stretching the limits of manpower. Leads poured in faster than they could process. A man claimed he'd seen a dark truck near a car wash. Another thought he recognized the driver from the sketch. Tips came from Dallas, Fort Worth, even Oklahoma.

Detectives followed them all. Most led nowhere.

They called in experts—behavioral analysts, FBI child abduction specialists. The team built a profile: a male, likely local, familiar with the area, opportunistic but calculating. Someone who acted on impulse but knew how to disappear.

That last part terrified them most.

Every hour without a break widened the gap. Every wrong turn meant the trail grew colder.

By noon on Sunday—less than twenty-four hours after the abduction—the story had gone national. CNN, ABC, NBC—all carried Amber's photo. Talk shows and radio stations urged listeners to call in tips. In a time before social media, word of mouth and television carried the burden of awareness.

The FBI expanded the search perimeter to include miles of rural land east of Arlington. Volunteers in pickup trucks drove slowly along country roads, scanning ditches and culverts. Farmers checked barns and sheds. Police officers knocked on doors until their knuckles bled.

In one nearby neighborhood, a woman walked the streets with a flashlight, whispering prayers as she searched. "I just kept thinking," she later said, "if it were my child, I'd want someone to look, even if it felt hopeless."

The sense of unity was overwhelming—and yet beneath it all, a creeping dread began to take root.

Because the one thing they didn't find was Amber.

By that evening, January 14, the tone at the command center had shifted. The initial adrenaline was giving way to exhaustion. Leads were tapering off, and with them, hope.

Simonds called a short meeting with his team. "We're not stopping," he told them, voice steady but eyes rimmed with fatigue. "Not until we find her."

They reviewed everything again: the time, the truck, the direction, the witness statement, the tire marks. There were no new clues—no ransom calls, no notes, no sign of life. Just silence.

And silence was the one thing they couldn't afford.

Outside, the night air was cold again. Reporters filed their stories.

Volunteers drifted home, promising to return at dawn. Donna stayed awake through it all, praying, whispering, bargaining with the heavens.

If you bring her back, I'll do anything. I'll never complain again. I'll give anything. Just please, let her be alive.

In the distance, a police siren wailed and faded, swallowed by the dark.

The first 24 hours had come and gone.

The world still didn't know where Amber Hagerman was—or who had taken her.

CHAPTER 5 THE CREEK

Four days after Amber Hagerman vanished, the search entered its fourth night — and hope was beginning to fracture under the weight of time.

Volunteers still gathered at the church each morning, their voices quieter now. The coffee pots brewed continuously. The flyers, once crisp and full of color, had begun to curl at the edges, weathered by wind and rain. Police still searched, but even the most seasoned officers felt it — that cold dread that comes when too many days pass without a trace.

Then, on **Wednesday, January 17, 1996**, at approximately 11:00 a.m., the call came in.

A man walking his dog along a narrow, trash-strewn creek bed less than five miles from where Amber had been abducted had seen something tangled in the reeds — something that shouldn't have been there.

He stepped closer, thinking it was a bag or debris. Then he saw a small hand.

The call went out over the radio. Officers arrived within minutes, sirens cutting through the stillness. The area, near Forest Hill Drive and Abrams Street, was partially hidden — a shallow drainage creek bordered by brush, broken glass, and bits of metal. To anyone driving by, it was just another forgotten patch of land.

Within the hour, it was a crime scene.

Detectives from Arlington Police and the FBI cordoned off the area with yellow tape. Reporters tried to get close, cameras rolling, but were pushed back. Helicopters hovered overhead. The winter air was heavy and wet, the kind that clings to clothes and memory alike.

When investigators reached the creek, they saw her.

The current was shallow, just a few inches deep, but cold. Amber's body had caught on a piece of debris near the embankment. She was partially clothed. The visible injuries left no room for doubt — this had not been an accident.

One detective would later describe the moment quietly:

"There are some scenes you don't forget. This was one of them."

The team worked silently, methodically. Every step mattered. The area was combed for evidence — footprints, fibers, tire tracks, anything that could tell them who had been there. Photographs were taken from every angle. The medical examiner was called to the scene.

As protocol demanded, one officer was assigned to notify the family.

When the knock came at the Whitson home, Donna Hagerman knew before she opened the door.

She had felt it coming — that creeping silence, that ache in her chest that refused to leave. The detective's eyes said everything. He didn't need to speak.

Donna screamed, her voice breaking the still air. Her mother caught her before she fell. Ricky, standing nearby, began to cry. It was a sound no neighbor would ever forget.

"She's gone," Donna kept saying. "Not my baby. Not my baby."

There are no words for that kind of loss. Only echoes.

At the creek, officers carried Amber's body out carefully, covered with a clean white sheet. Dozens of people — police, journalists, volunteers — stood in silence as she was lifted onto the stretcher. No one spoke.

For four days, an entire city had searched for a missing child. Now, they were witnessing the end of that search.

The body was transported to the Tarrant County Medical Examiner's Office. There, under sterile light, the truth began to take shape.

The autopsy confirmed what detectives already feared: Amber Hagerman had been **sexually assaulted and murdered**. Her throat had been cut. She had likely been killed two days before she was found.

It was brutal, deliberate, and senseless.

Even veteran investigators wept.

Back at the police station, the tone of the case shifted instantly. What had been a missing-person investigation was now a homicide. Evidence from the abduction site and the creek was re-examined, logged, compared. Fibers, fingerprints, hair samples —

all sent to the lab.

But technology in 1996 was primitive by today's standards. DNA testing was slow and limited. Trace evidence could take weeks, even months, to analyze. Still, detectives clung to every thread.

The truck became the focal point again — the dark pickup that vanished down Abram Street. The problem was, there were thousands of similar vehicles in North Texas. Leads poured in faster than the department could process them.

A reward was announced. The FBI offered additional resources. Police urged the public:

"Someone knows something. Someone saw that truck."

But days turned to weeks. The tips grew fewer. The outrage grew louder.

At Amber's funeral, the small church overflowed. Hundreds stood outside in the cold, holding candles and stuffed animals, faces streaked with tears. Reporters filmed quietly from a distance, their lenses fogged by the cold air.

Donna spoke through trembling lips. "I just want whoever did this to know," she said, "that you didn't just take my daughter. You took my heart."

She promised then and there that she would never stop fighting — not only for justice for Amber, but for every child who might one day need help.

Her grief, raw and unending, would soon fuel a national movement. But in that moment, she was just a mother burying her nine-year-old daughter.

The choir sang softly. The casket, small and white, was lowered into the ground. The sound of shovels against dirt was the only thing that followed.

Afterward, when the reporters packed up and the volunteers went home, Arlington tried to return to normal. But it never truly did. The lot where Amber had been taken remained cordoned off for days. Children no longer rode their bikes there. Parents no longer let them out of sight.

The police case board, once filled with hope, was now lined with evidence photos. A map with red circles. A list of possible suspects. A reminder that the monster who had done this was still out there.

Detectives worked around the clock, but leads dried up. Every day without progress was another wound in the heart of a community that had believed it could protect its own.

Amber's pink bike, now logged as evidence, sat in a police storage unit — the final artifact of a stolen childhood.

The creek was drained and searched again in the days that followed. Nothing new was found. But that place — a muddy, forgotten strip of water — became sacred ground.

Neighbors began leaving flowers and small white crosses along its bank. Someone placed a photo of Amber there, laminated and nailed to a wooden post. Beneath it, a hand-painted sign read:

"Justice for Amber."

It has never been taken down.

In time, investigators would come to understand that this case, brutal and unsolved, would ripple far beyond that small Texas town. That from the darkness of that creek, something powerful would rise — a system that would one day bear her name and save thousands of others.

But on that cold January day in 1996, all anyone could see was a mother's grief, a town's broken heart, and a question that still remains unanswered:

Who killed Amber Hagerman?

CHAPTER 6 EDGES OF CERTAINTY

In homicide work, grief has to make room for procedure.

Once the tears dry and the cameras fade, what remains is evidence — and evidence doesn't weep. It waits.

For detectives in the **Amber Hagerman** case, the hours and days following the discovery of her body became a meticulous race against contamination and decay. Everything had to be catalogued, labeled, preserved — because one day, one microscopic detail might speak louder than a thousand interviews.

The forensics team worked for hours at the creek where Amber was found. The area was cordoned off tighter than ever. Each movement was deliberate: photographs at every angle, markers placed beside footprints, soil samples collected where the ground had been disturbed.

The cold January air made the work harder. Mud clung to boots; hands numbed through gloves. Still, they pressed on. They collected **fibers**, **hair samples**, **trace soil**, and **organic material** from both the water and the bank.

The creek wasn't kind to evidence. The water had washed away much of what might have remained — fingerprints, skin cells, even footprints blurred by the flow. But in that mess of debris, the forensic team believed there might still be something worth saving.

They sealed each sample in sterile bags, labeled with time and location. These would be sent to the state lab in Austin and the FBI lab in Quantico.

Every vial, every swab, every tiny fragment was handled like gold. Because, in truth, it was.

Inside the Tarrant County Medical Examiner's Office, the autopsy room was silent except for the low hum of fluorescent lights. The chief medical examiner conducted the examination personally. The findings were grim: Amber had died of **cutting injuries to the throat**, consistent with deliberate violence. She had also been **sexually assaulted**.

The estimated time of death placed it roughly two days before her body was found — meaning she had been alive, held somewhere, for at least a short time after her abduction.

That single fact changed everything.

The killer hadn't just acted in a sudden burst of violence; he had control, opportunity, and time. Whoever he was, he knew how to move unseen.

The question that haunted investigators most wasn't only *who* had killed her — but *where* she had been kept.

Detectives worked side by side with the forensic analysts, combing through every item recovered from the creek. The **clothing fragments**, the **fibers**, the **debris caught in the folds of fabric** — each was logged, bagged, and sent for examination.

This was 1996, a transitional moment in forensic science. DNA testing existed, but it was still primitive. To extract a genetic profile required a large, clean sample — far more than a trace left behind on damp fabric. Partial profiles were often inconclusive, and there were no national databases yet linking offenders the way CODIS would a few years later.

Still, the scientists tried. They processed what they could, running tests that might have seemed miraculous just a decade earlier.

The results were frustratingly vague. There was DNA — but it was **degraded**, **partial**, and **insufficient** for identification. It could confirm a male presence but not a name.

One lab report, according to detectives, described the evidence as "promising, but not probative." In plain terms: it meant hope without direction.

Meanwhile, back at the Arlington Police Department, evidence filled entire rooms.

Maps, photographs, sketches, logs, the pink bicycle, Amber's clothing — each tagged and stored in sealed lockers. Officers were forbidden from discussing details outside of official reports. They knew that one leak, one rumor, could send the case spiraling into chaos.

A dedicated evidence custodian was assigned to the case, ensuring the chain of custody would never be broken. Every time a sample moved from one lab to another, it was logged, signed, and sealed again.

Years later, that caution would prove critical. Those same sealed bags — stored for decades — would become the foundation for future DNA testing that hadn't yet been invented.

Back then, though, it was like trying to build a bridge across a foggy river. They could see the other side — truth, justice, answers — but had no way to cross it yet.

Detectives also searched for environmental clues. The **creek** itself became an object of study: its flow pattern, depth, the direction debris moved. They wanted to know whether Amber had been killed there or placed there afterward.

The findings suggested she had been *dumped*, not killed, at that location. The area showed no signs of a struggle. That meant the killer had transported her — in a vehicle — and deliberately chosen a quiet, secluded site within minutes of the abduction scene.

That narrowed the suspect pool slightly. The perpetrator had to know the area well enough to find that spot without hesitation. Someone local. Someone familiar with Arlington's backroads and creeks.

But familiarity also meant invisibility. In neighborhoods like this, people knew faces, not names. A truck seen once might be forgotten by morning.

Forensics could only take the investigation so far. Beyond the evidence, detectives turned to behavioral analysis. The FBI's child abduction experts in Quantico built a **criminal profile**:

- Male, likely between **25–40 years old**.
- **Lives or works within 5 miles** of the abduction site.

- **Drives a dark pickup truck**, possibly older model.
- May have **changed his behavior** after the crime — leaving town, selling his vehicle, avoiding local news.
- Likely **acted alone**, motivated by sexual compulsion and opportunism.

The profile was chillingly generic — fitting hundreds of men in the surrounding area. But it gave investigators direction. They cross-referenced local offenders, parolees, and anyone previously charged with crimes against children.

Dozens were interviewed. None matched.

Weeks passed. Forensics trickled back with small findings — a few trace materials, inconclusive hair comparisons, environmental residue suggesting partial transport by vehicle. But nothing that could lead to an arrest.

The case file thickened by the day. The evidence remained locked away, like the truth itself — close enough to feel, too fragile to hold.

In the quiet moments between interviews, detectives stared at the photographs pinned to the board: Amber's school picture beside the map of Arlington, the composite sketch of a man who seemed to stare back without mercy.

They had science, but not certainty. They had evidence, but no suspect. They had grief, but no closure.

And so the case entered its next stage — the long, suffocating wait.

What no one knew then was that the samples sealed in those sterile bags would outlive everyone in that room. That decades later, as DNA technology advanced beyond what anyone in 1996 could imagine, those same traces might still hold the answer.

Science would catch up to the crime — eventually.

But in that winter of 1996, the men and women searching for Amber Hagerman were left staring into the edges of certainty, trying to find justice in the space between what they knew and what they could never yet prove.

CHAPTER 7 THE TRUCK AND THE MAN

For weeks after Amber Hagerman's murder, everything revolved around the truck.

Every tip, every late-night call, every witness statement circled back to the same question: **Who was driving the dark pickup that took her?**

It was both the most vivid and most maddening clue in the case — solid enough to anchor hope, vague enough to drown in it.

Detectives had a description: a **black or dark blue pickup truck**, possibly a **single-cab, short-bed model**, with **clear windows and no visible markings**. It had been seen speeding away from the abandoned grocery store parking lot at 3:18 p.m. on January 13.

But beyond that, nothing was certain.

Some witnesses thought they saw a **white decal or stripe** near the rear fender. Others swore the truck had **a chrome bumper**. One even claimed the tailgate was missing. The inconsistencies weren't lies — they were the distortion of trauma. Memory bends under panic.

The FBI's forensic sketch artist refined the image based on composite statements: a dark pickup, male driver, medium build, possibly short hair. The sketch was broadcast across every news station in Texas. Tips flooded in from as far as Louisiana and Oklahoma.

Each one meant another long night of phone calls, another drive down another dead-end road.

At the Arlington Police Department, a wall in the command center became known as *The Truck Board.*

Pinned across it were dozens of photographs: similar models — Ford Rangers, Chevy Silverados, Dodge Dakotas — each crossed out in red marker as they were cleared.

Detectives began checking **vehicle registrations** within a ten-mile radius of the abduction site. That meant **thousands** of trucks. Too many to chase all at once.

So they narrowed it down:

- Men living alone.
- Criminal records involving children or sexual violence.
- Owners who suddenly sold or repainted their vehicles after January 13.

The list shrank to a few hundred. Still overwhelming, but manageable. Teams split up, knocking on doors, inspecting garages, scanning driveways for fresh paint or new license plates.

"Half of Arlington drives a dark pickup," one detective muttered. "We're drowning in black trucks."

But they kept going, because somewhere among those was the one that mattered.

Meanwhile, FBI behavioral analysts revisited the **profile** of the suspect — "The Man."

He was likely local, they said. Someone comfortable navigating the residential streets and knowing which shortcuts to take to vanish. He might have had a **job that allowed him to blend in** — a contractor, mechanic, delivery worker, anyone whose truck would never raise suspicion.

They believed the abduction was **opportunistic but premeditated** — meaning the offender had fantasized about it, maybe even prowled the area before, but acted the moment opportunity struck.

He would have been **confident, brazen**, capable of abducting a child in broad daylight without hesitation. That suggested experience — perhaps previous crimes that hadn't been caught or reported.

After the murder, he likely **changed his routine**. He might have suddenly quit his job, moved away, or withdrawn from friends. Some offenders like this relive the crime privately — revisiting the location, keeping souvenirs, following news coverage obsessively.

Detectives wondered how many men in Arlington fit that pattern. Too many to count.

The **tips** kept coming. A dark pickup spotted behind a strip mall. Another seen idling by an elementary school. One caller claimed a co-worker had suddenly repainted his truck red.

Police followed them all.

One lead sent them to a junkyard outside Grand Prairie, where an old Ford truck had been scrapped just days after the murder.

Forensics dusted every inch of metal for prints, tested fibers, searched the cab for DNA. Nothing matched Amber's case.

Another tip led them to a man who'd been arrested years earlier for attempting to lure a child into his truck. He was interrogated for hours, polygraphed, released. His alibi held.

Each false lead stung more than the last.

"You start to feel like you're chasing a ghost," one detective said later. "A ghost in a pickup."

Donna Hagerman followed the investigation obsessively. Every time she saw a dark truck drive past her home, her stomach clenched. She found herself staring at license plates, memorizing numbers, half-convinced that one day she'd see *the* truck — the one from her nightmares.

"I used to dream about it," she said later. "About chasing that truck down. I'd wake up running."

She kept close contact with detectives, calling often, asking if there was progress. The answer was always the same: *We're working on it.*

But work doesn't always mean movement.

In early February 1996, a month after Amber's abduction, the case entered a stalemate.

The truck, once the center of the investigation, had become its black hole — swallowing every clue, offering none in return.

Detectives began expanding outward, looking beyond Arlington. They consulted **state vehicle theft databases**, **DMV repaint records**, and even **used car dealers** who might have seen someone anxious to trade in a vehicle matching the description.

The FBI issued a **BOLO (Be On the Lookout)** across multiple states. Still nothing.

The man and his truck had simply vanished.

What haunted investigators most was the speed — eight seconds. That meant precision. Control. The abductor knew exactly what he was doing. He didn't hesitate. He didn't panic.

That kind of confidence doesn't come from nowhere.

Some began to believe the man had done this before.

If true, that meant he might do it again.

The team reviewed **unsolved child abduction cases** across Texas — San Antonio, Waco, Houston — looking for patterns. There were similarities, but nothing conclusive. Different counties, different jurisdictions, different rules for evidence. Connecting them was like stitching smoke.

The case was growing colder by the day, and yet something in every detective refused to let go.

"Amber was ours," one officer said quietly. "We were supposed to protect her."

That spring, the reward fund grew. Local businesses, private donors, and the FBI contributed. Billboards went up showing the composite sketch beside a dark pickup silhouette and the words:

WHO KILLED AMBER HAGERMAN?

CALL 817-459-5646.

But the phone rarely rang anymore.

The sketch, once a symbol of urgency, had begun to fade from the public mind. People moved on. News cycles shifted.

Except for Donna. She didn't move on — she transformed. Her grief hardened into purpose.

If the man in the truck could vanish, she decided, then no other child should be allowed to.

It was from that conviction, and that loss, that the next phase of Amber's legacy would rise — a system designed so that the world could never look away again.

But before that could happen, investigators still had to stare down an unthinkable truth:

The truck was gone. The man was gone. And so was justice.

CHAPTER 8 THE FAMILY UNDER LIGHTS

When the cameras came, they didn't ask permission.

They never do.

By the morning after Amber's body was found, **East Abram Street** had turned into a scene of floodlights, news vans, and microphones. The yellow tape still flapped in the wind, and beyond it, a mother stood in the center of a nightmare that belonged to her — and yet, suddenly, to everyone.

Donna Hagerman had barely slept since the abduction. Now, the media waited outside her parents' house, cameras aimed at the front door like weapons. Every time she stepped outside, flashbulbs ignited. The world wanted answers she didn't have.

Reporters shouted questions:

"Do you believe the killer was local?"

"What message do you want to send?"

"How does it feel, knowing this could have been prevented?"

Donna didn't shout back. She didn't collapse. She stood there, eyes swollen, voice trembling, and spoke the only truth she knew.

"She was my baby. She was just riding her bike. I just want them to find the man who did this."

The microphones caught every syllable. Within hours, her words played on national television. America saw not just a story, but a face — a mother's face, raw and unfiltered, asking for justice.

Inside the house, grief hung in the air like a heavy fog.

Amber's room remained untouched. Her pink comforter still neatly tucked, her drawings taped to the walls. Her favorite doll sat on the pillow — waiting, as if unaware that waiting was now all anyone could do.

Donna walked into that room often in those first days after the funeral. Sometimes she'd sit on the bed and talk aloud, as though Amber could hear. "You're safe now, baby," she'd whisper. "Mama's going to make sure they don't forget you."

Her mother, **Glenda Whitson**, watched her daughter crumble under the weight of public grief. She tried to protect Donna from the relentless news cycle, but the world had already claimed Amber's story.

Each newscast replayed the same footage — the bike, the creek, the mother's face. It was empathy at first. Then curiosity. Then spectacle.

By the end of January, it had become something else: a national fixation.

The **Hagerman family** had always been private, humble people. They weren't used to speaking into microphones or facing cameras. But grief changes a person's vocabulary.

Donna found herself repeating the same words to every reporter, every detective, every stranger who asked: "Please, if you know anything, come forward."

She'd look straight into the camera lens, as if speaking directly to the man who'd taken her daughter. "You can't hide forever," she said. "God sees what you did."

It was part fury, part faith, part desperation — and it resonated. Viewers around the country saw in Donna not just a mother's grief, but a courage born of pain.

People sent letters from every state — sympathy cards, prayers, even small donations folded into envelopes with handwritten notes: *For Amber's justice.*

The cameras followed Donna everywhere. When she went to buy groceries, they waited in the parking lot. When she attended vigils, they filmed her tears. She had become the unwilling public face of parental terror.

Her privacy was gone, but she decided something else could take its place — **purpose**.

"I can't bring Amber back," she said to her mother one night, voice breaking. "But maybe I can stop this from happening to someone else."

It was more than grief talking. It was conviction beginning to take root.

She started reaching out — to victim advocates, to police, to community leaders. She wanted to know why, in the hours after Amber's abduction, the public hadn't been alerted immediately. Why weren't television and radio stations interrupted to warn people that a child had been taken in broad daylight?

The more she asked, the angrier she became.

Because no one had an answer.

By February, the media frenzy had begun to fade. The national spotlight, fickle and hungry, turned elsewhere. But Donna's voice didn't fade with it. She gave interviews, not because she wanted to relive her pain, but because she wanted people to remember Amber as more than a headline.

"She loved animals," she told one reporter. "She loved helping people. She wanted to be a teacher. She was so full of life."

The interviewer paused, camera rolling silently. "What do you want people to know about her now?"

Donna looked down for a moment, her hands trembling in her lap. Then she said softly,

"That her life meant something. That something good will come out of this."

It wasn't just a mother's wish — it was the seed of a revolution.

The community of Arlington refused to let Amber's story die quietly. Candlelight vigils continued weekly. Churches opened their doors for prayer services. Flyers stayed taped to gas pumps and telephone poles long after the tape turned yellow.

At night, Donna would step outside, stare up at the stars, and talk to her daughter. "You're still with me," she'd whisper. "I'll make sure they remember you."

She didn't know it yet, but those promises — whispered into the Texas night — would one day echo through sirens, phone alerts, and broadcast interruptions around the world.

But for now, under the relentless glare of camera lights and public scrutiny, she was just a mother trying to make sense of the unthinkable.

In time, the house on East Abram grew quiet again. The reporters left. The police updates slowed. The calls from the detectives became less frequent.

But the emptiness didn't fade.

Amber's photos still lined the mantel — smiling, forever nine years old. Her brother Ricky, once cheerful and talkative, grew quieter, his innocence dulled by what he'd seen. The family tried to keep living, but there was always an empty chair, an empty bike, an empty future.

Donna had learned something brutal: when the cameras leave, grief doesn't. It just gets quieter — and heavier.

Yet even in that silence, a fire remained.

One mother's grief was about to change how the world responded to a missing child.

CHAPTER 9 THE CITY THAT WOULD'NT FORGET

In most towns, tragedies fade with time.

But in Arlington, *time stopped* on January 13, 1996 — and no one wanted it to start again until something changed.

The murder of Amber Hagerman didn't just leave a family shattered; it left an entire city raw. People who had never met the Hagermans felt the loss as if it were their own. Parents stopped letting their children ride bikes past dusk. Neighbors left porch lights burning through the night. Strangers nodded to each other at grocery stores, united by unspoken fear.

But out of that fear came something else — **resolve**.

Arlington decided it would not be the city where a little girl died for nothing.

At first, it began with small acts.

Local churches organized prayer vigils. Schools held assemblies about safety and awareness. Amber's classmates made cards and hung pink ribbons on the playground fence.

At the corner of East Abram Street and the old Winn-Dixie parking lot, people began leaving flowers, stuffed animals, and hand-painted signs. The spot became an unofficial memorial. Some came to pray. Some just came to stand in silence.

One sign read:

"We couldn't save you, but we'll save the next one."

It was more than a sentiment. It was a vow.

Community leaders and police officers started meeting quietly in the weeks after the funeral. They had all seen the same pattern: the public's outcry, the desperate search, the endless tips that came too late.

Among them was **Richard Hagerman**, Amber's grandfather, a quiet man who had lost not only a granddaughter but a piece of himself. He asked a question that cut through the room like a blade:

"Why didn't every person in this city know she'd been taken the second it happened?"

There was no good answer.

The reality was simple and horrifying: in 1996, there was **no system** in place to alert the public immediately when a child was abducted. Police had phone lines and fax machines. TV and radio stations received information hours later — if at all.

By the time most of Arlington knew Amber was missing, the truck was long gone.

That realization struck a chord with a local woman named **Dianne Simone**, a mother and ordinary citizen who had been following the case closely. She called into a local radio station with an idea:

"If we can interrupt programming for weather alerts," she said, "why not for child abductions?"

That call — one spontaneous moment of outrage mixed with hope — would become the spark that lit the fire.

Within weeks, Simone's idea began circulating among local broadcasters and police officials. The concept was simple: create an **emergency broadcast system** for abducted children.

The early discussions were informal — just phone calls, meetings over coffee, notes scribbled on notepads. But the vision was clear: use the same technology that warned of tornadoes and storms to warn about something far more urgent — a missing child whose life depended on speed.

The Arlington Police Department, with the support of local radio stations, began working out the logistics. How would alerts be verified? How fast could information be shared? Who would decide what qualified as an alert?

It wasn't perfect at first. There were technical barriers, bureaucratic delays, and endless debates. But the determination was stronger than the red tape.

When the system was finally tested later that year, there was only one possible name for it.

They called it the **AMBER Plan** —

in memory of a little girl whose bike had been left behind in an empty lot.

The first local AMBER Alerts were crude by modern standards — simple bulletins broadcast by radio DJs and faxed to local newsrooms. But they worked.

Within the first few years, **multiple children were found alive** because of the quick mobilization the system allowed. When listeners heard the alerts, they looked out their windows, scanned parking lots, memorized license plates. The community itself became part of the search.

What had started as one mother's grief and one woman's idea was now saving lives.

Donna Hagerman, still grieving but resolute, attended early meetings about the program. She gave interviews supporting its expansion, standing in front of microphones once again — but this time, her pain had direction.

"If one child comes home because of this," she said, "then Amber didn't die for nothing."

As the years passed, the AMBER Plan spread beyond Arlington. Neighboring cities adopted it. Then counties. Then the entire state of Texas.

By 2002, it had gone national — officially named the **AMBER Alert System** by the U.S. Department of Justice. What began as a single community's heartbreak became a network spanning every state, later evolving into cell phone alerts, highway signs, and digital notifications that could reach millions in seconds.

Each time that familiar chime sounds — the piercing tone, the words *"AMBER Alert: Child Abduction"* flashing across screens — it carries more than information. It carries a legacy.

A legacy born from a creek, a bicycle, and a promise.

In Arlington, that legacy remains tangible. The memorial on Abram Street still stands, adorned with flowers and pink ribbons that fade and are replaced again each year. Locals still remember the day the sirens first blared for a child not as a warning, but as a vow.

Every January, families gather there to light candles and say her name. They pray not only for justice — which has yet to come — but for every child who was found because of her.

And somewhere, perhaps, in the quiet moments between prayers, they whisper a thank-you to the little girl who changed how the world listens.

Because Amber Hagerman's voice — though silenced — still calls out every time an alert is issued.

And somewhere, another child gets to come home.

CHAPTER 10 ECHOES THROUGH TIME

Time, they say, heals all wounds.

But in Arlington, time only carved the wound deeper.

Each January, as another year passes, the memory of **Amber Hagerman** rises again — in news reports, candlelight vigils, and the quiet prayers of a mother who still sets flowers on her daughter's grave.

Nineteen ninety-six is no longer a headline. It's a scar.

But scars, even when they fade, still tell stories.

For detectives who worked the original case, Amber was never filed away as "cold." Her name remained written on the whiteboard in the **Arlington Police Department's Major Crimes Unit** long after other cases came and went.

Every few years, a new detective inherited the case file —

thousands of pages thick, bound in heavy boxes, filled with photographs, transcripts, and evidence logs. Each time, they started over. Each time, they hoped that the next fingerprint, the next DNA advance, the next tip might be the one.

But so far, it never has been.

The case remains **open and unsolved** — a shadow at the edge of every conversation about justice and time.

Detective **Ben Lopez**, who took over the case in the 2000s, once described the files as "a living thing."

"You open it, and it breathes. It takes over the room. You feel her there."

In the evidence room, sealed boxes still hold the original clothing, soil samples, and the partial DNA profile that has lingered on the edge of resolution for decades. Modern technology has transformed what was once impossible into potential.

In recent years, forensic genealogists have revisited the samples, hoping that **genetic genealogy** — the same method that unmasked the Golden State Killer — might one day identify the man who took Amber's life.

But degraded evidence is a stubborn enemy.

The creek water that once washed over her body also washed away clarity.

Even so, police have said publicly that they "will never close the case." Each generation of detectives vows to keep her file open until science — or conscience — gives them a name.

The Hagerman family has lived with that uncertainty for nearly three decades. Donna's hair has silvered; Ricky has grown into adulthood. Every January, the anniversary brings both mourning and momentum.

At memorial events, Donna still speaks — her voice steadier now, though the ache never left it.

"He's still out there somewhere," she says. "But so is Amber's voice. Every time you hear that alert, you're hearing her."

Her life became the embodiment of that mission. She worked with local advocacy groups, helped raise awareness about missing children, and comforted parents who found themselves walking the same impossible path.

To some, she is still "Amber's mother."

But to others — to thousands of families who found their children because of the AMBER Alert — she is something more: proof that grief can become purpose.

In Arlington, the physical reminders remain.

The old Winn-Dixie lot is gone, redeveloped into something new. But those who know the story never forget what stood there — or what was lost there.

A few miles away, the small creek where Amber's body was found still flows, quiet and indifferent. Locals say it feels different there — heavy, haunted. Every year, new flowers appear along its bank, left by strangers who never knew her but know her name.

A plaque nearby reads:

"In memory of Amber Hagerman — May her light guide every lost child home."

It's not just sentiment. It's scripture for a community that still believes justice, like faith, doesn't expire.

The impact of Amber's story has long outgrown Arlington's

borders.

As of today, **over 1,000 children in the United States** have been safely recovered thanks to the AMBER Alert system — and thousands more worldwide through international adaptations.

Her name has become synonymous with rescue, urgency, and hope.

And yet, beneath that triumph lies the unsolved crime that started it all — the wound beneath the legacy. The paradox of Amber Hagerman is that she both changed the world and was betrayed by it.

The system born from her death has saved countless others.

But not her.

That truth still haunts every investigator who's touched her file.

When asked years later what justice would mean to her, Donna didn't hesitate.

"Justice isn't just finding who did it," she said. "It's making sure what happened to Amber never happens again."

Her words have echoed in congressional hearings, in law enforcement conferences, in classrooms, and through every phone that blares the piercing tone of an AMBER Alert.

Each alert is a heartbeat — hers, still pulsing through time.

There are crimes that destroy.

And there are crimes that, even in their cruelty, plant something indestructible in the human heart.

Amber's story is both.

The man who took her has yet to be found. His name remains

hidden behind the silence of time and the imperfections of science. But Amber's name — once whispered in grief — now travels across satellites and screens, summoning strangers to act, to notice, to care.

In that sense, she is not gone.

She became the warning that saves.

The echo that answers.

The voice that never went quiet.

EPILOGUE

—The Light That Never Fades

There's a photograph of Amber Hagerman that has traveled farther than she ever did in life.

She's smiling, her hair pulled back, her denim vest buttoned neatly over a white shirt — a nine-year-old girl who looks ready for the fourth grade, for birthdays, for everything still ahead.

It's the image that appeared on every news screen, every poster, every plea.

It's also the image that, decades later, still reminds the world what was stolen — and what was given back through her name.

Amber never lived to see how the world changed because of her.

She never knew that her story would cross borders, languages, and generations. That because of her, sirens would sound in distant cities, warning that a child was in danger. That her name would become both a cry and a command: **Find them. Now.**

Since the system's inception, **over a thousand children** in the United States alone have been rescued through AMBER Alerts.

Thousands more across Europe, Asia, and South America owe their safety to programs modeled after it — all carrying the same promise that began in Arlington, Texas.

Her legacy is not a monument or a plaque. It's motion — the rush of people who pull over on highways, scan license plates, share alerts, and act without hesitation because a sound on their phone reminds them of one girl who didn't come home.

For her mother, Donna, the years have softened nothing.

The pain never left; it only changed shape.

She still visits the cemetery, sometimes alone, sometimes with her grown son Ricky. She brushes leaves from the headstone and speaks softly, telling Amber about the lives she's touched, the children saved, the strangers who still write to say thank you.

"I always told you, baby," she whispers, "Mama wouldn't let them forget."

And she didn't.

Through interviews, advocacy, and sheer persistence, Donna helped turn grief into global awareness. She pushed for technology, training, and faster communication between police and the public. Her voice — trembling but unyielding — became part of the alert system's heartbeat.

When an AMBER Alert sounds, it carries both her daughter's name and her mother's will.

The investigators who once searched the creeks and alleys of Arlington have long since retired, but they still talk about Amber.

They remember the bicycle, the pink handlebar ribbons, the witness who shouted too late, the map filled with red circles.

Some still keep a copy of her photo on their desks, faded now from sunlight. It's not just a reminder of the case they couldn't close — it's a promise that they never will.

Every few years, technology offers a new glimmer of hope —

improved DNA sequencing, genetic genealogy, databases that didn't exist in 1996. Each advancement brings the same question back to life: *Could this be the one that finally names him?*

The evidence remains safe, waiting, as if even science refuses to forget her.

There's a strange balance in Amber's legacy — a mixture of light and shadow, loss and salvation.

Her killer remains unknown. Yet her name has saved more lives than any conviction ever could.

Her story began in a moment of horror, but it has ended in countless moments of redemption — every time a missing child is found, every time an alert interrupts regular programming, every time a parent's nightmare is cut short because the world was watching this time.

The world didn't save Amber.

But Amber helped the world learn how to save its children.

At dusk, the memorial near the old Winn-Dixie parking lot still glows with candles and pink ribbons. Some nights, a stranger stops there, not to cry but to remember.

They read her name. They whisper a prayer. And when they drive home, they leave the porch light on.

Because Amber Hagerman's story is no longer just about what was lost — it's about what remains: the light of a child who taught the world to listen faster, to look harder, and to never again let silence win.

Her voice — silenced once — now echoes through every chime, every alert, every life brought home.

And that echo is eternal.

A PERSONAL REQUEST

Thank you for reading **Blood at the Border: The Murder of Amber Hagerman.**

If this book resonated with you, I would be deeply grateful if you left a written review. Even selecting a star rating—without writing anything further—helps more than you might realize, as it signals to bookstores and platforms that this story matters.

If you'd like to leave a review, you can visit the Amazon page here:

Blood at the Border: The Murder of Amber Hagerman

Or simply scan the QR code below to go directly to the review page:

Your support helps ensure Amber Hagerman's story—and the stories of other victims like her—are not forgotten.

With gratitude,

Linda Davidson

ALSO BY LINDA DAVIDSON

ABOUT THE AUTHOR

Linda Davidson is a true crime author who writes for readers who want more than shock value — they want truth with a heartbeat.

She focuses on the kinds of stories that stay with you long after the news cameras leave: unsolved murders, missing persons, rural disappearances, and investigations that never received clear answers. Instead of chasing sensational headlines, Linda writes with one question in mind: *How can I honor the victim and still tell the full truth of what happened?*

In each book, she blends careful research, clear timelines, and compassionate storytelling. Readers are guided through evidence, leads, theories, and dead ends in a way that is easy to follow and emotionally grounded. Her work keeps the victim at the center of the narrative while also examining the failures, gaps, and human decisions that shaped each case.

Linda's books are written for true crime readers who care about people, not just plot twists. She writes for those who feel frustrated by shallow coverage and are hungry for deeper, more thoughtful explorations of the cases that haunt them.

Her promise is simple:

She will research carefully.

She will explain clearly.

She will tell the truth with respect.

She will never forget that the people she writes about were real.

Linda Davidson is a true crime author dedicated to telling

the stories others forget. She writes about unsolved murders, mysterious disappearances, and cold cases with a focus on the victims, their families, and the communities left behind. Combining deep research with compassionate storytelling, she helps readers make sense of complex investigations without losing sight of the human beings at the center of every case.

END NOTE

— *Light in the Dark*

Stories like this one walk us through some of the darkest places a human heart can go. It is easy to believe that evil has the last word—that violence, corruption, or indifference are stronger than anything else.

The Bible says something different. It tells us that God sees every unseen hurt, hears every unheard prayer, and judges every hidden deed. It also says that no life is beyond His reach, and no story is too broken to be redeemed. Justice matters to God. So does mercy. So does you.

If what you've read has stirred fear, anger, or regret in your own heart, know this: the door back to Him is never closed. Repentance is simply turning around and letting Him meet you where you are.

"Do not be overcome by evil, but overcome evil with good."

— Romans 12:21

"The light shines in the darkness, and the darkness has not overcome it."

— John 1:5

May these pages not only expose what went wrong, but also awaken a hunger for what is right—for justice, for truth, and for the kind of grace that can still save a soul.

DISCLAIMER

This book is a work of narrative nonfiction. It is based on publicly available records, law enforcement statements, court documents, media reports, and historical sources concerning the abduction and murder of Amber Hagerman.

Every effort has been made to present the facts accurately and responsibly. Where direct documentation is unavailable, certain scenes, descriptions, or dialogue have been reconstructed from verified accounts and contemporaneous reporting for narrative clarity. Such reconstructions are not intended to misrepresent events, but to help readers understand the sequence and human impact of the case.

This book does not claim to resolve the case or identify a perpetrator. Any discussion of persons of interest, investigative theories, or contextual analysis is presented solely for informational purposes and reflects publicly reported information at the time of writing. No individual is accused beyond what has been formally established by law.

The author has taken care to avoid speculation, sensationalism, or unnecessary detail, particularly given the nature of the crime and the age of the victim. This work is written with respect for the victim, her family, and all those affected.

This book is not affiliated with, endorsed by, or sponsored by any law enforcement agency, government body, or advocacy organization referenced within.

Reader discretion is advised.

ACKNOWLEDGMENTS

This book exists because a little girl's life mattered—and because so many people refused to let her story disappear into silence.

First and foremost, I acknowledge **Amber Hagerman**, whose life was taken far too soon. This book was written with the deepest respect for her memory, and with the understanding that behind every headline is a child who was loved, known, and irreplaceable.

To the **Hagerman family**, and to all families who have endured the unimaginable loss of a child: your strength, courage, and perseverance stand at the center of this story. No words can soften the weight of grief, but your willingness to speak, to remember, and to demand better has changed the world in ways few could have imagined. Amber's legacy endures because you refused to let her name fade.

I extend my gratitude to the **law enforcement officers, investigators, forensic specialists, and analysts** who have carried this case across decades. Many of you worked in silence, under scrutiny, and without resolution—yet you never closed the file. Your persistence reflects a truth too often overlooked: justice is not only measured by arrests, but by the refusal to forget.

To the **journalists, broadcasters, and researchers** whose early reporting preserved the historical record of this case: your work provided the foundation on which this narrative stands. Accurate reporting—especially in moments of chaos—matters. Without it, truth erodes.

I also acknowledge the **advocates, educators, broadcasters, and community members** who helped transform loss into action.

The creation and expansion of the AMBER Alert system stands as one of the most powerful examples of how public vigilance, technological innovation, and moral urgency can save lives. Every child brought home because of that system carries Amber's name forward.

To the professionals and organizations who work daily in **child protection, victim advocacy, and trauma-informed care**: your work often happens far from public view, but its impact is profound. This book is written in recognition of your efforts to protect dignity where it is most vulnerable.

Finally, to the **readers**: thank you for choosing to engage with this story thoughtfully and responsibly. True crime demands more than curiosity—it requires care, restraint, and a willingness to sit with uncomfortable truths. By reading with intention, you become part of the collective memory that keeps cases alive and voices heard.

May this book serve not only as a record of what was lost, but as a reminder of what can still be protected.

REFERENCES

1. Arlington Police Department. (1996). *Incident and investigative summaries related to the abduction and murder of Amber Hagerman* [Public records]. City of Arlington, Texas.

2. Federal Bureau of Investigation. (1996). *Child abduction response and investigative assistance in the Amber Hagerman case* [Law enforcement records]. U.S. Department of Justice.

3. Hagerman, D. (1996–2005). Public statements and interviews regarding the abduction and murder of Amber Hagerman. Various broadcast and print media archives.

4. National Center for Missing & Exploited Children. (n.d.). *AMBER Alert: History and impact*. Retrieved January 18, 2026, from https://www.missingkids.org/ourwork/amber

5. Office of Juvenile Justice and Delinquency Prevention. (2002). *AMBER Alert: A comprehensive guide*. U.S. Department of Justice. https://ojjdp.ojp.gov/sites/g/files/xyckuh176/files/media/document/amberalertcomprehensiveguide.pdf

6. Simone, D. (1996). Radio broadcast commentary on emergency child abduction alerts [Broadcast transcript]. Dallas–Fort Worth radio archives.

7. Texas Department of Public Safety. (n.d.). *Texas AMBER Alert system overview*. Retrieved January 18, 2026, from https://www.dps.texas.gov/section/intelligence-counterterrorism/amber-alert

8. U.S. Department of Justice. (n.d.). *AMBER Alert program overview*. Retrieved January 18, 2026, from https://amberalert.ojp.gov

9. Washington Post Staff. (1996, January 18). Texas girl found slain; killing sparks national outrage. *The Washington Post*.

10. Wikipedia contributors. (n.d.). *Murder of Amber Hagerman*. In *Wikipedia*. Retrieved January 18, 2026, from https://en.wikipedia.org/wiki/Murder_of_Amber_Hagerman